DOUGLAS CORPORATION BUSES

IN PICTURES

Centenary Edition

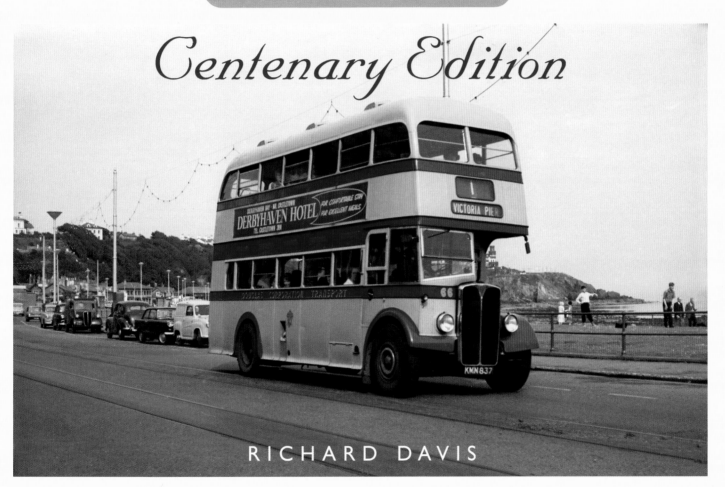

RICHARD DAVIS

Lily Publications

Published by
Lily Publications Ltd
PO Box 33, Ramsey, Isle of Man, IM99 4LP
Tel: +44 (0) 1624 898446
www.lilypublications.co.uk

Introduction

2014 marks the centenary of Douglas Corporation's motor bus services with their distinctive yellow livery and smart appearance, once a familiar sight on the roads in and around the Island's capital.

Giving an excellent and comprehensive service to locals and visitors alike from 1914 until nationalisation in October 1976, Douglas Corporation buses were a source of great pride to Douglas residents and of considerable interest to transport enthusiasts because of the often unique combinations of chassis and body not found in the fleet of any other operator.

As a preservationist and restorer of buses for more years than I care to remember, it has been a great privilege to have met many members of Douglas Corporation Transport staff at all levels. The one thing that came across loud and clear in my conversations with them was their dedicated professionalism and the quite rightly justified sense of pride in the bus fleet they all had a part in operating. I hope this volume will go some way towards recognising and recording their valuable service to the Island's capital over many years.

For those who remember Douglas buses, I hope that this book will act as a pleasant reminder of 'the good old days'. For those of you who may have moved to the Island subsequent to the demise of the Corporation fleet or are too young to remember it, then I trust you will find this glimpse of transport of a bygone era both interesting and entertaining.

Richard Davis

Photographs note: Images for the book were sourced from the author's collection (AC), Stan Basnett (SB), Travel Lens Photographic (TLP), the late Bill Lambden's collection (WTL), and the Keig Collection courtesy of Lily Publications (KC).

AEC Regent IIIs Nos. 56, 70 and 68 with St Barnabas Church as a backdrop. *(AC)*

Public transport consists of horse-drawn vehicles only in this 1880s scene at the bottom of Victoria Street. (KC)

Although the Manx Electric Railway had operated a pair of Argus charabancs from 1907 between the Bungalow and the company's tea rooms at Tholt-y-Will, no motor omnibus services existed on the Island's roads until 1914.

Previously, in addition to horse-drawn buses, Douglas was served by horse trams on the bay tramway and the Upper Douglas Cable Car system. This continued to operate until 1929 from the depot in York Road, the building then becoming the Corporation's bus depot.

While an all-Island bus service did not commence until 1927, Douglas Corporation Tramways had motor bus services under consideration for more than a year before commencing services in July 1914 - an operation that was to last for 62 years and which, many believe, marked an era of public transport on the Island that has yet to be surpassed.

In the early years of the 20th century, the Island's capital had a comparatively small local population of approximately 20,000 but a very significant number of visitors annually. Passenger arrivals on the Island are recorded as being over half a million just before the outbreak of World War I and peaking again just before and shortly after World War II with figures in excess of 600,000.

While not all holidaymakers stayed in Douglas, this gave transport undertakings in general, and Douglas in particular, a difficult task to cater for such wide variations. It was not until comparatively recent times, with the decline of tourism on the Island, that this enormous seasonal disparity virtually disappeared.

Douglas Corporation Tramways' first two buses were a Tilling-Stevens petrol-electric and a Straker-Squire, both seating 25. The Tilling arrived first and entered service at the end of July 1914 while the Straker-Squire, destined to be the only one of its type in the fleet, was delivered a few days later.

It had been anticipated that the buses would have been available to provide a summer service for the 1914 season but their delivery was delayed and within days of the commencement of bus services, World War I broke out. This effectively prevented any further deliveries and some six years were to pass before the first two buses were joined by a further four Tilling-Stevens.

Tilling-Stevens No. I at Peveril Square soon after delivery. The Victoria Pier Arcade is visible in the left background with the Peveril Hotel behind the bus. *(WTL)*

Above: Straker-Squire No. 2, MN 590 pictured in its original short-lived blue livery. *(TLP)*
Below: A view in the yard behind York Road Depot - showing an offside view of a Tilling-Stevens featuring an advert for Lawrence Wright, a prolific song writer and music publisher. *(WTL)*

7

As the accompanying photographs show, early deliveries came with solid rubber tyres and these gave a fairly bumpy ride on some surfaces.

What appears to be a wooden fence between the axles was present on most buses up to and including the 1950s and was quite simply a dog-guard rail. There being no legislation at the time to control unsupervised dogs, the guard rails were standard equipment designed to discourage the numerous free-roaming dogs from running under the moving vehicles. From 1922 to 1930, an additional 34 buses entered service, including the first double-decker, an open-top Tilling-Stevens, in 1926.

Often referred to as 'Tinkling Tillings' because of their musical

One of the early Tilling-Stevens poses in the depot yard off Waverley Road. Notices advising 'Standing Passengers Not Allowed' are prominently displayed on the side windows. (WTL)

engine/transmission note, Tilling-Stevens employed a pioneering system whereby a petrol engine drove a dynamo which in turn powered an electric motor drive to the rear axle.

Despite their somewhat lack-lustre performance in climbing the likes of Prospect Hill, the petrol-electric concept evidently met with the Corporation's approval because they went on to buy no fewer than 38 Tilling-Stevens of various models between 1914 and 1930, several continuing into service until 1949.

In May 1932, the Tramways Manager Steve Robinson - also the first bus service manager, retired and was succeeded by Cyril Wolsey who was destined to become Britain's longest serving Transport Manager, remaining in office until 1961. Very shortly after Wolsey's

Ten of the then twelve-strong Douglas Corporation Tramways fleet of motor buses lined up at Belle Vue. The newest, second from the left, is MN 3377, entering the fleet in 1924. *(SB)*

Former Douglas Corporation Tramways' Tilling-Stevens No. 10, a model TS3A with 26-seater bodywork by Tilling was new in 1923. After withdrawal from service in 1935, the bus was sold for non-PSV use and converted into a generator unit in 1938. Still retaining solid rubber tyres, it was acquired for preservation in 1957, the chassis, minus body, went initially to Clapham Transport Museum before becoming an exhibit at the Science Museum. This photograph appears to have been taken while the bus was awaiting removal of the bodywork and preparation for display. *(WTL)*

arrival, the transport undertaking was re-titled from the original branding of 'Douglas Corporation Tramways' to 'Douglas Corporation Transport'. Under Wolsey's management, the Corporation fleet continued to flourish and modernise and, as we will see, even the difficulties and deprivations of the Second World War delayed progress only comparatively briefly.

1933 marked the advent of the first buses from AEC (Associated Equipment Company) when two Regent I double-deckers with

Tilling-Stevens No. 12, MN 3377, with the crew standing alongside, pauses at Governor's Bridge during the Circular Tour. *(SB)*

Northern Counties bodywork arrived. These were also the first of many Corporation buses fitted with a pre-selector gearbox coupled to a fluid flywheel.

Further deliveries of Regent Is appeared over the next few years bringing the total to 10 by 1939. Early pictures of the Regent Is show the buses without a route number box. The first vehicle to be so equipped from new, Regent I, No. 50, did not arrive until 1939, the others having route numbers added later.

11

One of the early Tilling-Stevens petrol electrics is captured in this view at the junction of Quarter Bridge Road/ Thorny Road/Tromode Road, probably taken about 1920. *(SB)*

Douglas Corporation Tramways' first double-decker was this Tilling-Stevens TS3A, new in 1922, receiving fleet number 8. The location is Waverley Road with the depot entrance to the left of the picture. Note the advert for the bus service to horse races at Belle Vue. *(TLP)*

Fitted with open 'toast rack' bodywork with seating for 27, this Vulcan entered the fleet in 1926 and is seen here passing the TT Race Grandstand on Glencrutchery Road as part of the Circular Route. Receiving fleet number 17, and named after Vulcan, the Roman god of fire, the bus carried a mascot depicting its namesake, complete with blacksmith's hammer, on the radiator. *(WTL)*

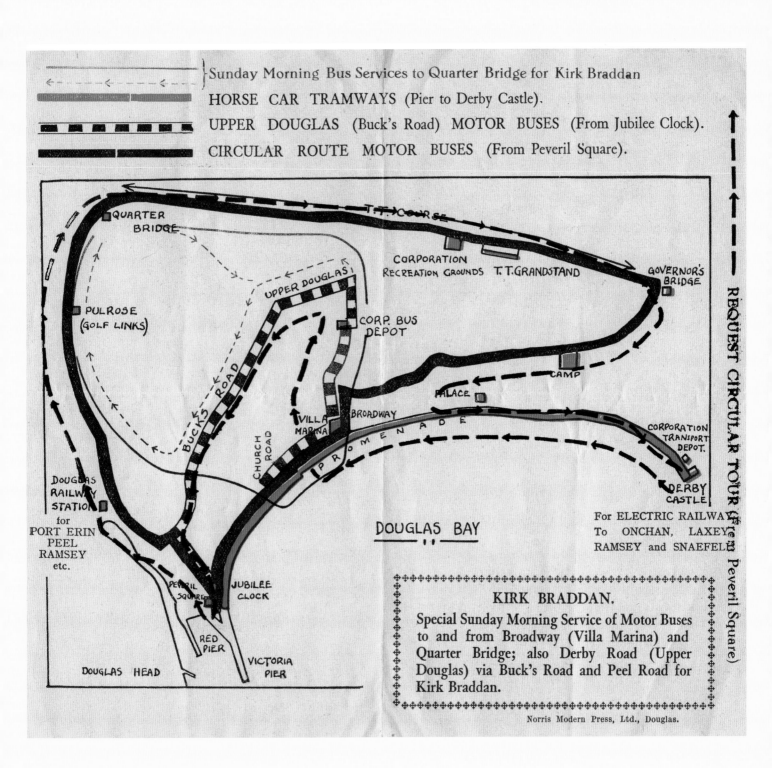

Sunday Morning Bus Services to Quarter Bridge for Kirk Braddan

HORSE CAR TRAMWAYS (Pier to Derby Castle).

UPPER DOUGLAS (Buck's Road) MOTOR BUSES (From Jubilee Clock).

CIRCULAR ROUTE MOTOR BUSES (From Peveril Square).

REQUEST CIRCULAR TOUR (from Peveril Square)

T. T. COURSE

QUARTER BRIDGE

GOVERNOR'S BRIDGE

CORPORATION RECREATION GROUNDS   T.T. GRANDSTAND

PULROSE (GOLF LINKS)

UPPER DOUGLAS

CORP. BUS DEPOT

CAMP

BUCK'S ROAD

PALACE

VILLA MARINA

BROADWAY

CORPORATION TRANSPORT DEPOT.

CHURCH ROAD

PROMENADE

DOUGLAS RAILWAY STATION

DERBY CASTLE

for
PORT ERIN
PEEL
RAMSEY
etc.

DOUGLAS BAY

For ELECTRIC RAILWAY
To ONCHAN, LAXEY
RAMSEY and SNAEFELL

PEVERIL SQUARE

JUBILEE CLOCK

RED PIER

VICTORIA PIER

DOUGLAS HEAD

✠✠✠✠✠✠✠✠✠✠✠✠✠✠✠✠✠✠✠✠✠✠✠✠✠✠✠✠✠✠✠✠✠✠
KIRK BRADDAN.
Special Sunday Morning Service of Motor Buses
to and from Broadway (Villa Marina) and
Quarter Bridge; also Derby Road (Upper
Douglas) via Buck's Road and Peel Road for
Kirk Braddan.
✠✠✠✠✠✠✠✠✠✠✠✠✠✠✠✠✠✠✠✠✠✠✠✠✠✠✠✠✠✠✠✠✠✠

Norris Modern Press, Ltd., Douglas.

The Circular Route as operated in the 1930s. *(AC)*

A manufacturer's photograph taken in the UK of 1930 Tilling-Stevens TS17A No.40, the last of the Tillings to be delivered. Fitted with pneumatic tyres from new and carrying 34-seater Northern Counties bodywork, 40 remained in service until late 1945. *(TLP)*

Again with bodywork by Northern Counties Motor and Engineering of Wigan, this Tilling-Stevens TS6, No. 25, was new in 1928 and lasted in service until 1949. Operating promenade route 1, the bus takes on passengers at the Strathallan Crescent terminus. By the time this photograph was taken, Cyril Wolsey had taken over as Manager from Steve Robinson, the 'Tramways' title had become 'Transport' and the DCT crest had been replaced by the full Corporation crest. Another notable feature is the addition of a route number box. *(TLP)*

Some of the eccentricities of the Regent Is are worth mentioning at this point - one of which was the strange trait of kicking the unwary driver in the left knee. For those unfamiliar with the technique of driving a pre-selector equipped vehicle a little information is called for. While these buses have the usual three pedal layout, the left one is not a clutch pedal but a change-speed pedal. The gear selector on the steering column can be moved at any time, regardless of engine or road speed, to the position of the next gear required and it is only when the gear-change pedal is pressed and released that the gear is actually engaged. However, and here is the catch - unless the pedal is pressed and released decisively it will often spring back forcefully and strike the unfortunate driver in the area of the left knee.

Ascending Douglas Head Road was therefore somewhat fraught as a downward gear-change was required near the bottom of the hill which was surfaced with granite sets that could jolt the vehicle quite badly. This often resulted in an imperfect gear-change and the resulting sharp reminder!

Another feature of the Regent Is, or rather lack of it, was the absence of a central vertical stanchion on the platform which was standard fitting for other double-deckers. This caused some minor inconvenience for passengers who were used to pulling themselves aboard with the aid of the centre pole. However, for one youthful conductor, this could have had dire consequences.

AEC Regent I rear entrance. Note the absence of a central vertical stanchion. *(SB)*

The lad in question, home from university for the summer and employed for the season as a conductor, had a trick of impressing the girls by running down the stairs from the upper deck and swinging out over the road while clutching the centre pole with his right arm, shouting out "Hi girls" to any attractive young ladies passing on the promenade nearby. You can imagine that his performance was less than impressive when he tried this one day while conducting a Regent I having completely forgotten that when he arrived on the open platform at some speed there would be nothing to grab hold of!

The first five AEC Regent Is lined up at Belle Vue - note the absence of route numbers which were added retrospectively. The fence in the foreground is part of the horse race track, discontinued in 1931. This location became King George V Park (now the NSC). *(SB)*

The first of the AEC Regent Is, No. 41, outside the Peveril Hotel. Prior to the arrival of fixed windscreens many years later, buses were equipped with opening cab windows as shown here. For the driver, sitting in an enclosed cab alongside what could be a hot engine, the breeze through the open window was very welcome on a warm summer day. Note the DTC crest on the side, later replaced by the more familiar Douglas Corporation coat of arms. *(WTL)*

Fortunately the bus wasn't travelling at any great speed and the resulting fall onto the road left him with nothing worse than a few bruises - and a slightly deflated ego one presumes...

At a time when there were numerous competing firms supplying bus bodywork, operators had considerable influence over the design and equipment of vehicles and would often issue detailed specifications to suit their own requirements rather than buying something 'off the peg'. The Regent Is, for example, were finished to a very high standard both externally and internally, with ornate flambeaux style interior lights, black plastic coated stanchions and white enamelled interior roof panels with walnut dividing strips.

It was during this period, from the middle 30s, that Douglas Corporation Transport started what was to become almost a trademark in choosing unusual chassis/body combinations. Possibly

Regent I No. 48 at Cambrian Place with St Barnabas Church in the background. The site hut suggests that this photograph was taken when demolition of the church was underway in the late 1960s. Note the semaphore indicator attached to the leading edge of the front lower deck window pillar. This type of indicator pre-dated flashing indicators and could sometimes be a bit problematic in either refusing to pop out when switched on or staying out when switched off. In many cases, up to the 1950s, buses were not equipped with any form of indicator and these were added later. (AC)

Insert: Interior light from a Regent I. (AC)

the strangest of these were two Vulcan single-deckers, new in 1935.

Although better known for its fleet of AEC buses, Douglas Corporation Transport acquired a number of Leyland buses over the years, the first of which were two Leyland Cubs with Park Royal bodywork arriving in 1936. These were capable of one-man operation and were followed by a further two in 1937 and one each in 1938 and 1939 giving a total of six. These proved to be particularly good buses, continuing in service until 1957-1959.

As it happens, the Cubs were very timely deliveries as the country was about to embark on another world war a mere 21 years after the end of World War I. This is where the Leyland Cubs came into their own as, even without power-assisted steering, they were

AEC Regent I, No. 48, on route 4 to White City via Derby Castle picks up passengers outside the Palace. (AC - photo by Len Hulme)

not as heavy to drive as many of the other members of the fleet.

Apart from the obvious and immediate impact upon tourism, other notable effects on the transport fleet soon became apparent as men were conscripted or volunteered for the armed forces and the Corporation initially employed four (later rising to seven) female driver/conductors, the last of whom did not finish their duties until November 1945.

One of the first effects of the war with its attendant blackout of lighting on vehicles, street lamps and buildings, was the hasty provision of curtains for the Douglas buses to prevent light showing outside the vehicle. This was done for all but six buses that could not be dealt with in the time available. The simple expedient for this was to paint

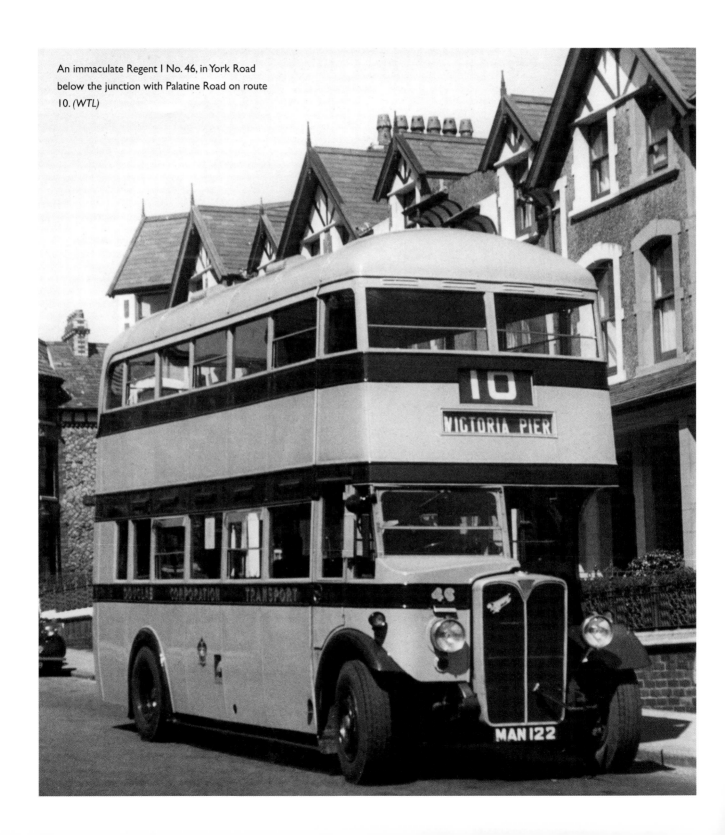

An immaculate Regent I No. 46, in York Road below the junction with Palatine Road on route 10. *(WTL)*

Right: In later years the Vulcans, Nos. 1 and 2 received Bedford radiators, engines and gearboxes, resulting in a marked change to their front-end appearance. *(TLP)*

Below: Vulcan No. 1 as delivered in 1935, complete with nearside folding doors and minus the route number box fitted later. The scene is Laureston Avenue, with York Road Depot to the right and Murray's Road School behind the wall on the left. The two Vulcans, Nos. 1 and 2, were some of the first buses delivered with the new fleet name 'Douglas Corporation Transport'. Note the advert in the windscreen for the Extended Circular Tour - Nine miles for 1/- (one shilling = 5p in today's money). *(WTL)*

Vulcan No. 2 alongside the Victoria Pier Arcade with the Peveril Hotel in the background. The Vulcan, which is on route 37 Railway Station shuttle service, still has the original front but with a route number box added.

This view only partially illustrates the intensity of bus services using the arcade as the other two sides would also have been in use. It is difficult to comprehend the volume of passenger arrivals and departures in the Island's heyday as a tourist resort until one considers an observation by Corporation Transport Manager Cyril Wolsey in 1938 that on August Saturdays there were 15 arrivals and 16 departures of Steam Packet ships during a 24 hour period. With the 2,000 plus passenger capacity of the ships, almost every bus in the fleet had to be pressed into service. *(AC)*

Bill Lambden collection

Pictured when new in 1939 and proudly displaying the Douglas Corporation crest, No. 14 was the last of the Leyland Cubs delivered and was a KPZ3 type, the previous deliveries having been KPZ1s. *(WTL)*

the windows of the buses which was a lot quicker and every bit as effective.

Another effect of the war was the lack of available new vehicles to replace older stock. This meant that vehicles that might have been disposed of earlier, such as the older Tilling-Stevens, were retained and kept running with limited resources in terms of both engineering staff and spare parts.

Despite the lack of tourism, the Corporation buses were kept busy during the war as there were large numbers of military personnel on the Island and they relied heavily on public transport to get about, as did the local population, restricted as they were by petrol rationing and other shortages.

Many of the major bus manufacturers had been obliged to switch their output from buses to military vehicles and war materials so the supply of new buses soon dried up. Eventually the UK Ministry of Supply gave in to demands from operators for replacement vehicles and some so-called 'utility' buses were produced.

In the Corporation's case, these came in the form of two Bedford OWB single-deckers in 1944 and three Daimler CWA6 double-deckers, right at the end of the war, in 1945. Though the vehicles were normal specification as regards the engine and chassis, all were fitted with austere utility bodywork by Duple. Today we would probably

Top: Driver's lapel badge. *(AC)*
Above: Conductor's leather bag. *(AC)*
Left top and below: Driver and Conductor metal cap badges *(AC)*

Leyland Cub No. 8 with
Bedford OWB No. 15 behind, at
Peveril Square. The driver/conductor
is equipped with a Bell Punch ticket
machine, leather cash bag and the ubiquitous
'T' key wedged behind the brass plate on the
bag. The T keys were used for opening 'budget
locks' often found on detachable or hinged
body panels and floor traps on the buses and
for unlocking the dummy clocks found in many
of the shelters. (WTL)

Leyland Cub No. 8 on route 14 outside Yates's Wine Lodge with a Road Services Leyland Titan PD1 emerging from Walpole Avenue. Further Corporation buses can be seen in the background at the side of the Victoria Pier Arcade. (WTL)

refer to these as 'no frills' due to the lack of refinements where cheaper materials such as steel instead of aluminium body panels were used and some fittings such as comfortable 'Dunlopillo' seat cushions and upholstery were replaced with wooden slatted seats more commonly found on a park bench!

Bedford OWBs were the only type of single-deck Utility bus produced and came with the standard 32-seat layout and wartime brown primer paintwork. The two examples purchased by the

Corporation were delivered with 32 seats but this was altered after their arrival on the Island and they only ever operated with 26 seats in order to conform to local regulations for one-man buses.

Following the end of hostilities, operators lost no time in ordering replacements for life-expired vehicles and Douglas Corporation Transport, no doubt eagerly anticipating the return of tourists to the Island, once more turned to AEC to provide what was to be the backbone of the post-war fleet with an eventual total of eighteen

Leyland Cub No. 8 followed by Regent III No. 71 catch the afternoon sun as they pass Gelling's Foundry on the way up Victoria Street on routes 14 and 11 respectively. (WTL)

Bedford OWB No. 15 on the shuttle service to Douglas Railway Station is seen alongside the Victoria Pier Arcade with Road Services' Leyland Titan PD2, No. 72, behind. *(AC)*

Regent III double-deckers.

The first two of these, Nos. 54 and 55, arrived in 1947 and were different to the ones that followed in that they were 'RT' types as used in large numbers by London Transport and proved to be the only RTs bodied by Northern Counties. The remainder, also with Northern Counties bodies, with minor variations, were standard Regent IIIs.

While both the RTs were withdrawn and scrapped at Manx Metals, Balthane in 1971, seven of the later Regent IIIs survived until the take over by Isle of Man National Transport in 1976. Despite them being issued with new fleet numbers, none of them were operated by the newly formed government undertaking and the majority were subsequently exported and eventually scrapped.

Subsequent deliveries of Regent IIIs saw four arrive in 1947 (56-

Bedford OWB No. 16 at Strathallan Crescent showing the tiny headlights fitted to wartime deliveries. These would have carried masks during World War II to prevent the headlights being seen by enemy aircraft, thus reducing the already feeble output even further. The plain and rather angular bodywork can be seen to good effect in this view. The use of an unseasoned timber frame with steel panels rather than aluminium and the reduced number of curves made the body cheaper and easier to produce, if a little less attractive to the eye. The Bedfords were not built with a long lifespan in mind but nevertheless, Nos. 15 and 16 lasted in service until 1957. *(WTL)*

Daimler CWA6 No. 52 is seen in Douglas Railway Station forecourt in July 1962 showing the wooden 'park-bench' type seating fitted to the wartime deliveries. These buses proved to be surprisingly good and were easy to maintain without the need for complex workshop equipment. All three lasted until in service until 1970. *(WTL)*

59), four in 1948 (60-63) and eight in 1949 (64-71).

It is interesting to note the developments in what were basically the same vehicle type as the bodymaker, Northern Counties of Wigan, made slight alterations to the specification.

For example, after No. 56 the windows varied between the sliding and half-drop type while different types of roof-mounted air vents could be observed between batches. The destination displays also had the side destination box moved from above the platform to the lower deck window from No. 64 onward and the last six delivered (Nos. 66-71) had rubber mounted route number and destination boxes and also the upper deck rear window, giving them

a less angular appearance.

Another modification involved AEC Regent III Nos. 58 and 60 being fitted with towing hitches, for towing horse trams, the only members of the fleet so equipped.

An incident involving Regent III, No. 62, is a testament to the resourcefulness of the engineering staff at York Road when the bus had the misfortune to suffer a mechanical failure on Prospect Hill causing it to mount the pavement and collide with Jim King's cycle shop on the corner of Athol Street. The resultant distortion was such that the body was removed by Corporation Transport staff and the chassis sent to the manufacturer for repairs before being returned to York Road Depot for re-assembly and return to service.

Generally speaking the Regent IIIs proved to be extremely suitable for the Douglas routes as they were easy to drive, being fitted with pre-selector gearboxes and air brakes. The fact that they had bodywork of 7 feet 6 inches width as opposed to the 8 feet (2.45 metres) of later models, enabled them to get through such traffic as there was without much difficulty.

The next deliveries were a complete contrast in that they were Leyland Comet single-deckers. Three of these, fitted with Park Royal bodywork and numbered 20-22, joined the fleet in 1950. The Comet was more familiar as a goods chassis and no other municipal operator in the UK operated them as a bus. The Comets were always the vehicle of choice when there was snow on the roads, as was often the case in winter in those days, and a couple of sets of spare wheels, with snow chains fitted ready for use, were always to be found hanging on brackets on the wall in the yard behind York Road depot.

A total change in the choice of single-deckers came the following year when two AEC Regal IVs arrived, both second-hand. These were

Still looking good in the summer sun, Daimler CWA6, No. 52, on Loch Promenade with Loch Parade Church, built in 1878 and replaced by a modern successor in 1976, in the left background on the corner of Howard Street. (AC)

Regent III RT No. 54 at Lord Street on the circular route 20. Note one of the dummy clocks in the shelter, the hands of which were altered by the conductor to show the time of the next bus. (AC)

AEC Regent III RT No. 54 descends Prospect Hill on route 14 from Ballabrooie to Victoria Pier, subsequently incorporated into route 36 in 1955. A once familiar sight at the bottom of Prospect Hill was that of the policeman on 'point' duty controlling the traffic which, at the time of the photograph, consisted of a five-way junction - all carrying two-way traffic. (WTL)

Regent III RT No. 55 about to depart on Circular route 20 from Peveril Square. The driver has just checked the destination, the conductor is on the platform while an Inspector, far right, keeps a watchful eye on things. *(WTL)*

AEC Regent III RTs Nos. 54 and 55 pictured together in front of the Peveril Hotel ready to operate the Circular Route 20 and 30 in opposite directions. The shallow radiator shell, low bonnet height, solid offside rear lower deck panel and uneven headlights can clearly be seen. Another modification involved the T shaped handles for raising and lowering the bonnet which were a feature of the RTs. These were replaced on the following Regent IIIs by a round knob which was less easy to grasp especially on wet days. *(WTL)*

as different as could be imagined from anything that had gone before, with engines mounted horizontally under the floor instead of at the front as had been the case for previous deliveries.

No. 30 had been displayed at the 1950 Commercial Motor Show and was originally intended for City of Oxford but they decided not to proceed with the purchase and it came instead to Douglas.

Regal IV No. 31, fitted with bodywork by Park Royal, had been an AEC demonstrator, new in 1950 and showed an interesting contrast in style for what were otherwise identical vehicles.

Douglas Corporation thereby acquired two fine vehicles in

Delivered later in 1947, No. 56 by contrast, has a deeper radiator cowl, equal-height headlamps, different front wings and windscreen, plus sliding windows as opposed to the 'half-drop' type on Nos. 54 and 55. As with many of the photographs used in the book this one illustrates the marked lack of traffic on the Island's roads at the time. (AC)

A summer Sunday scene on Peel Road with a queue of passengers returning to town on route 8 from the very popular open-air church service at Kirk Braddan. The number of people attending required Isle of Man Railways to operate special trains to Braddan Bridge Halt and it was not unusual to see more than twenty coaches unloading passengers in Saddle Road. *(WTL)*

Lower deck interior shot of Regent III No. 68. Note the 'treadmaster' ribbed rubber flooring. On bus No.63 this was incorrectly fitted across the gangway for a time making it thoroughly disliked by cleaners as it was very difficult to sweep out. *(AC)*

Regent III No. 60 emerging from the York Road paint shop with double-deck horse tram 14 in tow ready to take part in the 1976 horse tram centenary. Note the sloping roof of the access to the cable pit which ran underground across York Road. During World War II, this was used as an air-raid shelter and later still as a rifle shooting range. *(SB)*

virtually new condition at a good discount. Both went on to give many years' service and were not retired until 1976 and 1974 respectively.

While no further new deliveries occurred for several years, commencing in 1954, the Corporation embarked on a conversion programme where several of the pre-war Regent Is had their petrol engines replaced by refurbished diesel units from scrapped London Transport STL-class double-deckers. This gave an immediate saving as the cost of diesel was at that time much cheaper than petrol, plus mileage per gallon of fuel just about doubled!

After the two Regals joined the fleet, there was a gap in deliveries until 1957 when another significant change occurred. This time it involved double-deckers in the form of four AEC Regent Vs. These were the first eight foot wide vehicles bought by the Corporation and were also the first fitted with what was termed 'mono-control', semi-automatic gearboxes. As it turned out, they were also the last rear-entrance buses acquired.

For those unfamiliar with semi-auto transmission, the main difference to preceding batches of vehicles was the absence of a third foot pedal, a brake and accelerator being all that was required, together with a miniature gear lever mounted on the left side of the steering column. Unlike the pre-selector gearboxes, the movement of the gear lever on the Mark Vs resulted in an almost instantaneous

engagement of the selected gear. A mechanical inhibitor was incorporated into the selector switch to prevent downward changes from fourth to second gears without going through third in the process and thereby over-speeding the engine.

The Regent Vs were something of a mixed blessing in that they had a good power-to-weight ratio - the unladen weight being over a ton less than later Mark Vs - but the extra six inches in width caused problems in passing horse trams on the promenade routes

AEC Regent III, No. 60, towing seven horse trams along Douglas Promenade in connection with the horse tram centenary in 1976. *(SB)*

and other vehicles at some locations. An incident on the Old Castletown Road near Ellenbrook when two eight footers on route 15 met on a narrow section of road resulted in one of them, travelling towards Port Soderick, slipping into the roadside ditch and falling against the hedge smashing some of the nearside lower deck windows.

Having light-weight bodywork but a reasonably powerful 9.6 litre engine and semi-automatic gearbox, the rear-entrance Regent Vs were probably a driver's dream but the lively performance had to be used with caution. For example, when the vehicle was accelerating hard up Lord Street from Quines Corner and across the Athol Street/Peel Road junction, anyone standing on the back platform had

to get a firm grip on the handrails or risk being thrown off due to the abrupt transition in road alignment at that point.

Also arriving into the fleet in 1957 were some more examples of the Corporation's taste for unusual vehicles in the shape of five Guy Otter single-deckers. These were very similar to London Transport's 'GS' (Guy Special) class of which they had 84 examples using Guy Vixen wagon chassis with Eastern Coachworks bodies. Douglas however, specified bodywork by Mulliner, again with massive destination boxes and destined to be the only Mulliner-bodied GSs supplied to any operator.

The Otters were quaint-looking vehicles but not the nicest to drive as the steering was heavy for such a small bus. The Perkins P6

Regent III No. 61 at the bottom of Bray Hill. The conductor has just been setting the dummy clock in the shelter used to indicate the time of the next bus into town. *(WTL)*

Left: The conductor of another Regent III alters the clock on Quarterbridge Road. *(WTL)*

Above: : Close-up of one of the clocks. *(AC)*

DOUGLAS CORPORATION TRANSPORT

OUR CORONATION
HOLIDAY PROGRAMME
1937

FARES CHEAPER !
FACILITIES BETTER !!
ATTRACTIONS GREATER !!!

PLEASE KEEP FOR REFERENCE DURING YOUR
HOLIDAY AND RETAIN AS A SOUVENIR FOR
YOUR FRIENDS.

SERVICES ON ALL ROUTES DURING
THE SUMMER MONTHS EVERY FEW
MINUTES

*All Tram and Bus Services connect with the
Steamers and Railways*

**EXTRA BUS SERVICE BETWEEN
STEAMERS AND
DOUGLAS RAILWAY STATION**

Circular Route

Attractive Saloon MOTOR BUSES leave
PEVERIL SQUARE (Victoria Pier) and
BROADWAY (Villa Marina) at FREQUENT
INTERVALS DAILY

✦✦✦

SPECIAL FEATURE —
The Circular Bus runs over
part of the T.T. Course

You can break your journey and enjoy a game
of Golf at PULROSE or Tennis, Bowls, Cricket
and Miniature Golf at the RECREATION
GROUNDS, and resume your travel later
ROUND RURAL DOUGLAS

"The Trip of the Season"

C. F. WOLSEY, A.M. Inst. T., General Manager.

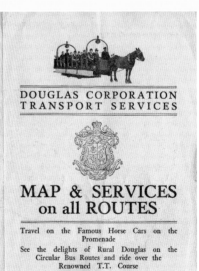

DOUGLAS CORPORATION
TRANSPORT SERVICES

MAP & SERVICES
on all ROUTES

Travel on the Famous Horse Cars on the
Promenade
See the delights of Rural Douglas on the
Circular Bus Routes and ride over the
Renowned T.T. Course

Transport Dept.
Strathallan Crescent   DOUGLAS.

A 1971 view of AEC Regent III, No. 65, returning to the town centre after a trip to Upper Douglas on route 12. The side destination box was moved from above the platform and inserted into the lower deck side window bay from No. 64 onward. No. 65 was one of the Regent IIIs that did not survive into the nationalised era, being withdrawn in 1974, three years after this photograph was taken. *(TLP)*

AEC Regent III, No. 69, awaits the next departure on route 25 to Douglas Head from Lord Street Bus Station. *(AC)*

AEC Regal IV, No. 30, at Lord Street Bus Station on route 32 to Governor's Bridge. Note the semaphore indicator on the offside front corner has failed to fully retract after its last use - a common problem with this type of 'trafficator'. *(AC)*

AEC Reliance No. 33 parked up between duties at Cambrian Place. The former ironmongers shop of Todhunter & Elliot is the white building in the centre background with the widows houses to the right. *(AC)*

Above: AEC Regent V, No. 1, on route 4 at White City. *(AC)*

Right: AEC Regent V, No. 2, illustrating the change of livery with the reduction of the red bands from three to one and simplified fleet name adopted in the early 1970s. *(AC)*

engine was noisy and the gear selection process could be entertaining as the gear lever positions were a mirror image of normal practice with first and second on the right and third and fourth on the left! Nevertheless, they were very rugged and simple vehicles, often to be found on the Port Soderick route 15, once a very popular destination for the crowds of tourists who flocked there by road, rail and sea. Single-deckers went via the Marine Drive and returned to town via the Old Castletown Road while double-deckers used the Old Castletown Road in both directions. All five Otters survived until 1970 when they were replaced by second-hand Leyland Tiger Cubs, several Otters subsequently being preserved in the UK.

From the comparatively agricultural Otter, the Corporation had another total change of direction in 1958 with the purchase of two AEC Reliance underfloor-engined single-deckers. Quite possibly the most successful AEC single-deck chassis produced, these two had AECs AH470 engines and semi-automatic transmission and were said to be a delight to drive. As might be expected, there was another

Subsequent to nationalisation, Isle of Man National Transport took over the Corporation's York Road Depot and here we see a Leyland National together with Leyland PD3 No.63 and former Douglas AEC Regent III No.56 in the sheds at the rear of the depot. The Regent had been sold for non-PSV use and converted to open top. (AC)

quirk in that they were given Mulliner bodywork - the only Reliance chassis to be so fitted anywhere in the world.

Following nationalisation, the two Reliances were absorbed into the amalgamated fleet but even though they were given new fleet numbers, 189 and 190, they never ran in service again and were soon withdrawn from stock and sold. Despite their unique chassis/body combination, both ended their days at Booth's scrap yard in Rotherham.

No further deliveries occurred until 1964 when three further AEC Regent V double-deckers arrived, this time with forward entrance MCW bodywork. Receiving fleet numbers 1-3, these were quite conventional vehicles for a change and were a good solid bus

A once familiar scene at the Victoria Pier Arcade: On the left, passengers wait with their bags for the next bus while on the street lamp is an advert for "Request Circular Tour, Open Buses Leave Here Every Afternoon & Evening. One Hour. Fare 1/3". To the right, a porter pulling a luggage cart precedes Utility Daimler CWA6, No. 52, which is on route 19 to Pulrose. Road Services' Leyland PD2, No. 79, and AEC Regent III, No. 65, wait by the arcade frontage while people enjoy the summer weather sitting outside the cafe. The arcade, with road access on all three sides, provided an

excellent facility for meeting the steamers as the following observation by Bill Lambden, who in August 1953, was on the staff of Bus & Coach magazine, reveals: 'The first boat came in at 4.50 am followed by six others in an hour, bringing a total of 12,255 passengers.' He continues, 'The Corporation had 20 double-deckers and five single-deckers, the latter mainly one-man operated, standing by at the pier heads from 4.30 am. On the Road Services, the duty inspectors had 14 double-deckers standing by.' *(WTL)*

Above: AEC Regent V, No.4 showing the yellow front applied to this bus and sister No.5, evidently done in error by the body-builder Willowbrook. A similar error was made in the painting of the two final Regents, Nos. 14 and 15, though in their cases the bonnet tops were painted red rather than yellow. *(AC)*

Right: Though also delivered with a yellow front, Regent V, No. 15, provides a comparison showing how the later repainting altered the appearances of the last four Regent Vs to be delivered. *(AC)*

VICTORIA PIER
BUS STATION

227 UMN

DOUGLAS CORPORATION TRANSPORT

PAY AS YOU ENTER

Ex-Lancashire United Leyland Tiger Cub No. 34 in York Road opposite the depot. (AC)

Former Douglas Corporation Transport AEC Regent Vs, repainted red and white and with new fleet numbers, in service with Isle of Man National Transport. *(AC)*

Above: Former DCT No. 6, Bedford VAS1 carrying Isle of Man National Transport legal lettering and fleet number 99 at Ramsey Bus Station, well outside its usual territory, following nationalisation in 1976. (AC)

Right: Ex-Douglas Corporation No.7 Bedford VAS1, repainted and renumbered in the National Transport fleet outside the former Isle of Man Road Services Homefield Depot. (AC)

Here, No. 70 shows the final Regent III body style as it enters Peveril Square with Walpole Avenue, Yates's Wine Lodge and the Villiers Hotel in the background. Note the police telephone pillar on the right, used for communication with Police HQ before the advent of police radios. *(AC)*

Leyland Comet No. 20, (minus fleet numbers) poses for an official photograph in the UK prior to delivery. *(WTL)*

A 1953 view of Leyland Comet No. 22 waiting to depart on route 5 to Ridgeway Road, Onchan. *(TLP)*

Above: A rare shot of Comet No. 20 about to cross the bottom of Bray Hill from Stoney Road on the short-lived route 17 to Tromode via Upper Douglas, discontinued in 1955. *(WTL)*

Below: Regal IV No. 30 shows off its Willlowbrook bodywork while parked facing the 'wrong way' at Lord Street with the Albert Hotel in the background. *(AC)*

AEC Regal IV, No. 30, on stand number 1 at Lord Street with Road Services' Leyland Titan PD2, No. 63, in the background. Note the leather cash bag and Gibson ticket machine carried by the conductor and the 'EA' (Extended Area) lettering below the nearside front sidelight. *(AC)*

Official photograph of AEC Regal IV No. 31 prior to delivery, looking very smart with its polished ribbed aluminium trim and chromed wheel trims. At this stage some of the fittings are still absent and a decidedly non-standard font has been used for the fleet name. *(WTL)*

AEC Regal IV, No.31, at Strathallan Crescent with the horse tram depot in the background. Most unusually for Douglas Corporation buses, the Park Royal bodywork is a bit the worse for wear in this view, as a result of a road accident in York Road, and in fact it was never fully repaired before the bus was withdrawn from service in 1974. (AC)

AEC Regal IV No. 31 in the turning bay at the route 25 terminus on Douglas Head. *(TLP)*

Regent V No. 75 emerges onto Lord Street from the bus station at the start of route 11 to Upper Douglas. By the time this photograph was taken, Ambrose Hampton had become the Manager, which dates the picture as 1969 or a little later. *(AC)*

in every respect.

Two additional Regent Vs, numbered 4 and 5 came in 1965, this time with Willowbrook bodywork incorporating sliding cab doors, and heralding a departure in livery style with an all-yellow front, bonnet top and nearside front wheelarch panel.

The next arrivals, in 1966, were two small Duple-bodied Bedford VAS1s. These took fleet numbers 6 and 7 and at only a shade over 4 tons, their acquisition may well have heralded the beginning of an economy drive by the Corporation as the transport undertaking was becoming increasingly costly to operate. In an attempt to make

savings, the VAS1s were ordered without heaters/demisters though this had to be remedied later when it was discovered that the windscreens 'fogged-up' and could not be kept clear.

1968 saw a final pair of double-deckers delivered. These were AEC Regent Vs of the 3D2RA type, again with Willowbrook bodywork but fitted with the larger AV691 engine of 11.3 litres. At over 8 tons unladen weight, these were the heaviest buses in the fleet, and also featured yellow fronts though in this case the bonnet tops were painted red. As it happens, the second of the two Regents, which became fleet number 15, was the last of its type built by the AEC company.

Regent V No. 75 has just returned from a trip to Willaston in this view taken at Parade Street/Bath Place junction with the Royalty Cinema in the background. As can be seen, the early Mark Vs featured a very large destination display with plenty of route information. This was all very well when it worked but all too often the blind would get creased or out of position resulting in a tangled and often largely illegible blind. Later pictures show these apertures drastically reduced to letter-box proportions to overcome the problem. *(AC)*

The last four Regent Vs (Nos. 4, 5, 14 and 15) gave the impression of being less sturdy than the preceding MCW-bodied examples (Nos. 1-3) and did not last as long in service, with some being withdrawn early due to defects. For example, Regent V No. 14 had to be withdrawn with failing bodywork while both No. 5 and No. 15 developed engine faults resulting in premature withdrawal from service. No. 15 was reinstated as a member of the 'heritage' fleet but with a smaller 9.6 litre engine in place of the original 11.3 litre unit.

There are a variety of reasons for the financial difficulties that both the Corporation and Road Services were experiencing at this time. Reducing visitor numbers for one, at least partially brought about by the increasing popularity of foreign holidays. Added to this, many holidaymakers now brought their own cars to the Island, something made much easier by the advent of car ferries operated by the Isle of Man Steam Packet Company. Couple this with rapidly rising car ownership of Manx residents and it is not hard to see why the bus companies were having to make economies.

When further vehicles were acquired in 1970, this was reflected in the purchase of eight second-hand Leyland Tiger Cubs from Lancashire United Transport taking fleet numbers 34-41. Ideally suited

Regent V No. 73 at the Sea Terminal showing the reduced destination display on both front and side. Several porters' handcarts can be seen on the extreme left of the picture. (AC)

AEC Regent V No. 74 at Lord Street Bus Station ready to depart on route 18 to Willaston. Note the 'EA' lettering below the offside front sidelight denoting a vehicle authorised to operate up to 2 miles beyond the borough boundary. *(AC)*

for expanding the Corporation's use of one-man-operated buses, the Tiger Cubs were new to LUT in 1957 and 1958 and it might be thought that they were well worn by the time they arrived in the Douglas fleet. However, great care had been taken by DCT engineers to obtain the best of what was available and these buses proved to be a good buy. Several of them operated through to nationalisation in 1976 and were undoubtedly capable of continuing in service beyond that.

Following the National Transport takeover, the surviving Tiger Cubs were quickly disposed of, all going for scrap to either local or UK dealers.

As an interesting aside, while York Road Depot normally carried a comprehensive range of spare parts for the buses, there would be an occasional time when the stores ran out of something needed

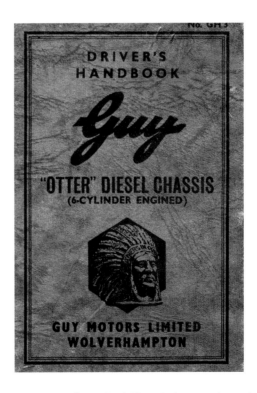

Above: Guy Otter driver's handbook. The vehicles carried a similar depiction of an Indian chief on the bonnet with the legend, 'Feathers In Our Cap'. *(AC)*

Left: Guy Otters Nos. 9 and 10, final inspection completed and ready for delivery from Mulliner's coachworks in 1957. *(WTL)*

Otter No. 12 at Strathallan Crescent. Note the projecting raised 'probe' on the nearside front wing, the purpose of which was to show the driver the position of the side of the bus since it could not be seen from the driver's seat. This earned the class the nickname of 'Sputniks' with some drivers after the Russian satellite launched in the same year - it had four protruding radio aerials! An alternative nick-name was 'Wolsey's Camels' on account of the two humps! *(AC)*

Guy Otter No. 10 at the junction of Lord Street and Parade Street. This bus passed to Ballamona Hospital upon withdrawal in 1970 and the photo shows the vehicle in the hospital's pale blue and red livery (note the absence of fleet name and number and the Corporation crest). In the background, the Steam Packet are advertising day trips to Dublin and Belfast for £2. *(TLP)*

AEC Reliance No. 32, looking very stylish when brand-new and still without fleet numbers, pictured at the handing-over ceremony outside Douglas Town Hall. This was once a familiar scene, the arrival of new buses being a matter of great civic pride and considerable public interest. Transport Manager, Cyril Wolsey is fourth from the right. *(TLP)*

AEC Reliance No. 33 in Lord Street - the background to this picture has since changed dramatically with many of the old buildings cleared away. As can be seen in this picture, the destination blind is developing a distinct curl on the offside. Towards the end of their life, the destination displays were much reduced in size to address this problem. *(AC)*

AEC Reliance No. 32 at Lord Street awaiting the next trip to Douglas Head. Note the very small rear-view mirrors with which these and other buses were equipped. Even by the late 1960s, things had not improved and many of the older vehicles were never fitted with more generously proportioned mirrors. *(AC)*

urgently to get one of the fleet back on the road. In such a case, it was not unusual for an apprentice to be dispatched on the morning ferry for a day trip to Liverpool to pick up the vital part from the AEC Depot at St. Helens or Joseph Lucas at Edge Lane.

As a general rule, and barring accident damage, the buses were repainted, by brush, every seven years with a touch-up and varnish about half way through the cycle. The ivory and black livery originally used soon gave way to the more familiar Primrose and Deep Red

giving the fleet a very clean and smart appearance. This work was undertaken in-house in the paint-shop which is seen on the extreme left of the depot photograph.

Along with Public Service Vehicles of other operators, the Corporation buses were subject to testing by the Isle of Man Highway & Transport Board examiners at the Quarter Bridge Yard (behind the hotel). Until the advent of 'rolling road' brake test equipment, brake testing was done during a road test with the aid of

Regent V No. 1 at Strathallan Crescent with a much more modest destination display than its predecessors. No. 1 was not only the first of the forward entrance Regent Vs but also became the very last former Douglas Corporation bus to be operated by Isle of Man National Transport, being finally withdrawn in October 1982. *(AC)*

a Tapley Meter, a mechanical device placed on the floor of the vehicle and used to indicate brake efficiency.

An acceptable brake reading could be difficult to obtain with certain types of bus, particularly the pre-war double-deckers, and this was often only possible if the brakes were adjusted so that there was barely any clearance between the brake shoes and the brake drums. This was all very well for testing but after a few brake applications, the friction surfaces would expand and cause the brakes to bind making it impossible to operate the bus in service. The simple solution was to adjust the brakes to get a good test reading and then drive the bus carefully to the Highway & Transport Depot with minimal use of the brakes. Having passed the test, the bus would then return to York Road where the brakes were de-adjusted so that it could run in service without binding brakes! This was overcome by

AEC Regent V No. 2 ready to depart from Lord Street on route 4 to White City (Onchan Head) via Derby Castle, with Leyland Tiger Cub No. 35 behind on route 36 to Ballabrooie. *(AC)*

A 1971 view of Laureston Avenue showing the difference in body width of Regent III, No.64 (left) and Regent V, No.2, (right). Note the flashing indicators within the waistband on 64 - a replacement for semaphore 'trafficators' added some years after the buses were delivered. Often used as temporary parking for buses taken out of the depot early in the morning to await collection by a driver, Laureston Avenue was the scene, some years previously, where an unattended Tilling-Stevens single-decker ran away and collided with one of the Murrays Road houses in the background - as it happens, the home of a Corporation Transport employee! *(TLP)*

Regent V, No. 5, departs from Lord Street on route 1 to Derby Castle. In the background, Fort Street, with the Steam Packet's works, runs off at an angle on the right while St Barnabas Church is prominent in the centre overlooking two Regent IIIs. *(AC)*

Regent V, No. 4, approaching Broadway after the yellow front had been repainted in conventional colours. *(AC)*

Bedford VAS1 No. 7 leaving Peveril Square with the Sea Terminal (lemon squeezer) in the background. *(AC)*

Bedford VAS1, No. 6, with AEC Regent V, No. 4, among others, parked up awaiting their next duty. Note the wheel chock positioned under the offside front wheel of No. 4. This was standard practice with Corporation buses fitted with pre-selector or semi-automatic gearboxes. The reason being that regardless of whether or not a gear was selected, the vehicle could still roll away in the event of the driver not setting the handbrake properly or handbrake failure - a rare but not unknown event. *(AC)*

Bedford VAS1 No. 7, though minus its fleet number in this scene, passes St Barnabas Church in Lord Street. Since the destination is blank, the bus may well have been on a private hire duty. *(TLP)*

Regent V No. 14 passes the Peveril Hotel with the Royalty Cinema behind and Lord Street Bus Station in the left background. In this view, 14 seems to have acquired a nasty gash on the centre red band at the offside rear corner. *(AC)*

Regent V No. 15 on route 4 to White City with its original yellow front livery during the summer of 1969. *(TLP)*

the fitment of automatic brake adjusters from the AEC Regent IIIs onward. However, brake problems were not quite at an end and some of the Regent Vs were discovered to have overly-sensitive footbrakes, resulting in a modification by the manufacturers to stop passengers being thrown forward when the brakes were applied.

While the next deliveries were to be new buses, again economies were made in specifying lightweight Bedford YRQs one of which, No. 16, arrived in 1974 with three more, Nos. 17-19 arriving early in 1975.

With the YRQs, further cost-savings were made - one of the features of the model being a single-cylinder air compressor as opposed to the more usual twin-cylinder type. The result was that the air-operated windscreen wipers could not be replied upon as the compressors were unable to keep up with demand - the brakes also being operated by air pressure. As a low-cost modification, the air wiper motors were replaced with electric wipers.

In addition, the traditional livery and lettering was simplified so that the block-shaded fleet name and number became a much

The last two AEC Regent Vs, Nos. 14 and 15, parked together at the route 4 White City terminus. On summer evenings, the combined capacity of the two double-deckers would be needed to ferry large numbers of holidaymakers between the town centre and this very popular attraction. Note the Majestic Hotel in the right background across Happy Valley. *(TLP)*

less impressive plain black font. Other members of the fleet were treated in similar fashion when they became due for a repaint, with a single red band being applied to the Regent V double-deckers.

By 1976, the future for both Douglas Corporation Transport and Isle of Man Road Services bus fleets was looking bleak, Road Services in particular being under severe financial pressure. The result of this was a merger of sorts, something which had been under discussion for ten years, and the two fleets were amalgamated under the government-owned Isle of Man National Transport Ltd banner on 1st October 1976.

Thus the final Bedford YRQ, delivered the previous year, became Douglas Corporation Transport's last ever bus bringing the total number of buses owned to 118 over the 62 year life of the undertaking.

Subsequent to the amalgamation of the two fleets, and despite their generally very good condition, many of the 32 former Corporation buses absorbed into IOM National Transport never ran again in public service. The bulk of them went to the UK, mostly to scrap dealers, with just a handful escaping into preservation or to non-PSV use.

Those that did operate in National Transport ownership often did so for a considerable period still wearing their Douglas colours but with hastily applied amended legal lettering on the nearside lower

The first of the Leyland Tiger Cubs, No. 34, in the depot yard off Waverley Road with other members of the Corporation fleet lurking in the gloomy confines of the sheds behind - a view rarely seen by members of the public. *(TLP)*

panels. Eventually, those that continued in use were repainted in National Transport red and white, sometimes running over former Road Services routes for which they were less than ideal because of their comparatively low top speed.

If nationalisation of the Island's bus fleets was meant to fix all the problems, it was a dismal failure as those who took on the management of the nationalised undertaking were in a no-win situation right from the start. There simply wasn't enough investment forthcoming from government and a variety of stop-gap measures, including the importation of numerous second-hand buses from the UK in the late 1970s and early 1980s, did little to help the situation.

Regent V No. 15 at the route 15 terminus at Port Soderick. Another once popular tourist destination with an attractive glen, hotel, children's paddling pool, smugglers' caves, oyster beds and amusement arcade. *(TLP)*

AEC Regent III No.68 looks in need of a good clean in this Lord Street view. Note the extended semaphore indicator just behind the driver's cab.
Authors note: Some years after it was withdrawn from service, I had the great pleasure of driving this bus for a considerable mileage in the UK. It was without doubt the finest Regent III I have ever driven. *(AC)*

Successive re-branding under a variety of names has failed to reverse the loss-making nature of bus operations on the Island. More importantly from the transport enthusiast's perspective, the Island's buses no longer have their historic appeal as they are much the same as can be experienced throughout most of the UK and Ireland.

Having said that, bus travellers and enthusiasts in the 1960s said exactly the same thing when AEC Regent Vs and Leyland PD3s replaced some of the older and arguably more interesting members of the Corporation and Road Services fleets. Some of the older vehicles that were retained mainly for seasonal use during the height of the summer certainly had character but they often presented difficulties and a distinct lack of comfort for passengers due to their steep steps, open rear platforms, lack of heaters and so forth.

An old type Tapley brake testing meter. *(AC)*

York Road Omnibus Depot, formerly the Upper Douglas Cable Car Depot. The bus fleet was garaged and maintained in York Road Depot and in sheds at the rear accessed via Waverley Road. Not only was the work done to a very high standard but, bearing in mind the fairly basic equipment, some heavy maintenance tasks were undertaken by Corporation engineers. *(WTL)*

Leyland Tiger Cub No. 36 has just made a right turn out of Broadway and heads along the promenade towards the Sea Terminal. The Duple bodywork with 'sun-windows' is seen to good effect in this shot. Note the Tiger Cub badge below the destination screen. Similar badges, featuring a raised enamel picture of the animal in question, often members of the cat family, were a familiar sight on many Leyland vehicles such as Leopard, Panther, Lion, Tiger etc. Though the vast majority of the buses have long since disappeared, many of the attractive badges have survived and often change hands for considerable sums of money among collectors. (AC)

A familiar scene at Cambrian Place featuring AEC Regent III No.58, Daimler CWA6 No.52 (with the inevitable wheel chock), AEC Regal IV No.30 and an unidentified AEC Regent I. *(AC)*